To Charlie.

Very Best Wishes!

Hope you enjoy the book...

Remi Milner

Richard / ~~[illegible]~~ Holly / Sarah John /

THE RIVERBANK GANG SPENDS CHRISTMAS

Written by Richard Wilmot

Illustrated by Howard Molloy

Richard J
Holly J
Sarah J
John J
Dom J
Amy C J
Amber J
Al
RIVERBANK

FOR DANIEL

Designed, produced and published by

Wilmot Bill Publishing Ltd.

Printed in the UK by Rapier Press Ltd.

STORY 1.

Christmas Eve

OLLY

Christmas Eve

It was Christmas Eve morning…a cold misty day,
On the riverbank you could hear a pin drop,
Just the faint sound of birds broke the silence far away,
And the chimes from an old village clock.
As Olly Otter peered out of his creaky front door,
Still aching from the previous night,
He couldn't believe the scene that he saw,
For everywhere was covered in white.
A carpet of snow about twelve inches thick,
Lay over the whole riverside,
"Whooppee! I'd better wake everyone quick,"
Olly yelled, with a grin a mile wide.
He just couldn't get dressed quickly enough,
He found an old scarf and woolly hat,
And last…from a drawer…and still covered in dust,
His snow shoes…two table-tennis bats!

He'd found the two bats a few months before,
And spent many hours making laces,
From some string he'd discovered washed up on the shore,
And the elastic from an old pair of braces.
He tied them on tight, his face flushed with pride,
'I <u>do</u> hope they work,' he kept thinking,
Then he opened his door and ventured outside,
"Yippee!" he could walk without sinking!

He was still dancing round when he heard a voice call,
"Olly!...It's Matty and Eel."
Matty Mole, Olly's best friend, was walking towards him,
"Well you wanted some snow, how d'you feel?"

"Great!" answered Olly, as he scooped up some snow,
Then rolling a ball behind his back,
He hurled it at Eel with an accurate throw,
That almost knocked his unsuspecting friend flat.

"Merry Christmas, you three!" shouted Skinny the Shrew,
As he wandered up dragging his sledge,
"Well," inquired Skinny, "you like it don't you?
I found it downstream in a hedge."

Skinny's sledge was the lid from a used biscuit tin,
"It's great, but a bit dangerous don't you feel?"
"Rubbish, Matty!" answered Skinny. "Come on you lot, get in,
And let's see what it's like down this hill!"

They all clambered on and sat behind one another,
Then Skinny took a hold of the rope,
But before they all knew it, the small sledge leapt forward,
And they were racing full speed down the slope.

"Look out, I can't stop!" shouted Skinny to Eel,
"You shouldn't have given such a push,"
But they sped even faster, flew over a hill,
Hit a bump...and landed splaat! in a bush!

They picked themselves up and brushed off the snow,
All four of them soaked to the skin,
"Well, that's quite enough of that! I know where we'll go,"
Matty groaned, as he rubbed his sore shin.

"To Chairman Frog's house, do you remember last week,
He had the most marvellous plan?
He said if it snowed enough this Christmas Eve,
We could all build a giant snowman!"

They trudged off together without more ado,
The snow coming well past their thighs,
All except Olly, whose trendy snow shoes
Were keeping him comfortable and dry.

When they reached Frog's home he was standing outside,
Puffing...and terribly red,
"Hello fellas! You can help me crack some of this ice,
Here, take hold of this shovel!" he said.
Frog's petrol tank home was frozen completely,
Long icicles hung from the door,
"I won't let a bit of cold weather defeat me,
But I've known nothing like this before."

Matty Mole soon took over poor Chairman Frog's spade,
A spoon from an old ice-cream tub,
While Frog watched his progress, looking somewhat amazed,
Groaning, "Olly...give my back a quick rub."

Before very long they had cleared a large space,
"This is perfect for the snowman!" shouted Eel,
"You're right," agreed Frog. "This **could** *be the place,*
But let's see how the others all feel!

So Matty, go and round up the rest of the gang,
And bring them here, there's a good lad,
Get Dan Dragonfly, Moorhen and Snake if you can,
Oh! And don't forget Rat or he'll go mad!"

Matty arrived at King Rat's house soon after,
Almost slipping on the snow near the door,
And as he told him the plan, Rat burst into laughter,
"What a spiffing idea!" he roared.

"I'll just get my coat and some warm, furry boots,
It looks pretty cold out to me,
And if we're building a snowman, I'll need some gloves too!
You know I'm not as young as I used to be!"

By just after lunch they'd all finally arrived,
Frog said, "Friends, Merry Christmas to you all!
We've had an idea that could be great fun,
So we decided to give everyone a call."

Frog explained about the snowman and everyone clapped,
"Sss..sss..superb," said Snake with a smile,
"Brilliant," Dan agreed, "but let's hurry you chaps,
'Cos it'll start getting dark in a while."

"Right," said Frog, "Matty, Skinny, Olly and Dan,
Make the snowman a body, you four,
Roll up the biggest snowball you possibly can,
Then stand it just here...by the door."

Moorhen and Eel, you're responsible for the head,
Snake...you find some pebbles for his eyes."
"What can I do?" asked Rat. "Oh, don't worry," Frog said,
"You and I will spring a little surprise."

The huge snowman began to take shape before long,
Its body all glistening and white,
"Now Matty," said Olly, "you can put the head on,
Here...stand on my shoulders if you like."
Snake had found two superb pebbles for the eyes,
And a small ice cream tub for a nose,
"Fellas...without wishing to criticise,"
Olly frowned, "Something's missing you know!"
Just then Chairman Frog and King Rat reappeared,
With a bag simply bursting with things,
When the others saw what was inside, they all cheered,
"These should make him look better," Frog grinned.
From out of the bag Frog first took a cloak,
Then a bow tie...then velvet top hat,
"And to finish him off," said Frog with a croak,
"A cigar...donated by Rat!"

"He's splendid!" smiled Rat, when the snowman was done,
"It's been a fantastic Christmas Eve,
Now let us all think about making for home,
But 'three cheers for Frog' before we leave!"
The animals yelled aloud, "Hip, Hip, Hooray!"
Then they all began collecting their things,
After all, in a few hours it would be Christmas Day,
And heaven knows what adventures would begin . . .

STORY 2.

Christmas Day

Christmas Day

At last Christmas Day had finally come,
Matty Mole was feeling very excited,
"Oh, I ***do*** *hope my party is going to be fun,*
It should be...everyone's been invited!"

Matty glanced round his home...he was proud as could be,
There were streamers...and cards...and balloons,
And to finish it off...a huge Christmas tree,
Sparkling brightly in the centre of the room.

Draped over the branches were a dozen blue candles,
Around the base...an enormous red bow,
"That tree," Matty thought, "was quite difficult to handle,
But I think it was worth it, you know!"

"Oh! The presents!" Matty yelled, "I almost forgot,"
And he dashed out once more from the room,
Then returned muttering, "Let's hope they like what I've got,
Well anyway, we'll know pretty soon!"

Suddenly, a very loud knocking outside
Made Matty jump out of his skin,
He rushed to the door and opened it wide,
"Merry Christmas everybody!...Come in!"

As his pals shuffled in, they all took off their shoes,
First Moorhen...then Skinny and Olly,
Then Snake, Eel and Rat...and, last, Dan wandered through,
Shaking snow from a small cocktail brolly.

"This place looks superb!" Olly muttered to Matty,
As he patted his friend on the back,
"What a wonderful tree!" "Oh yes...very natty!"
Murmured Dan, "Where on earth d'you get that?"

"Oh that!" answered Matty "it was quite easy really,
I just carried it home...on my head."
"By yourself?" said Olly stunned, "but it's bigger than me!
My dear boy, you must be half dead."

They all giggled, then Matty raising his glass,
Said, "To us...and our Riverbank home!"
He was just about to sip when he suddenly asked,
"Wait a minute!...Where's Frog?...Didn't he come?"

Sure enough, the rest of his pals were all there,
But Chairman Frog was nowhere to be seen,
"Well, we can't start without him, it wouldn't be fair,"
Moorhen nodded, "Yes...it is a bit mean."

As they stood round the fire, working out what to do,
A strange noise suddenly came from outside,
They all rushed to the window to get a good view,
"Whoever can it be?" Skinny cried.

Outside in the garden, ankle-deep in the snow,
A large, rounded figure appeared,
He was dressed all in scarlet from his head to his toes,
And he wore a long, fluffy, white beard.

"Good grief! ... It's Father Christmas!" yelled Dan to the rest,
"It is, too!" nodded Skinny and Eel,
"Fffather Christmas!!," stammered Snake (really impressed),
"But I didn't think Father Christmas was real!"

Matty opened the door, very slowly at first,
"Ccccan I help you?" he nervously inquired,
"Yes, I've dragged this big sackful of presents for miles,
Can I come in?...I'm getting quite tired!"

The stranger's deep voice sounded slightly familiar,
He put down his bulging, brown sack,
Then blowing on his hands said, "The weather's turned chillier
And I left my sleigh a couple of miles back!"

Rat suddenly laughed...and started winking at Dan,
Who was perched in the corner, on a log,
"Well! You almost fooled me for a minute, old man,
BUT I'D KNOW THAT VOICE ANYWHERE...

MM

...FROG!!"

All the animals looked at each other...then grinned,
"It's Frog! Chairman Frog!" Matty sighed,
"You'd better tell Snake...what a tizzy he's in,
He's gone to the kitchen to hide!"

Before long, Frog had thrown his disguise on the floor,
And he was drinking and looking relaxed,
"You should've seen your faces when you opened that door!",
Frog spluttered, "I nearly collapsed!"

"Well," now, Matty called, "I've got a surprise,
I've hidden your presents all around,
But they've all got your names on, so open your eyes,
And just yell when the last one's been found."

The animals began searching, under cushions, behind chairs,
"Here's mine, in this bucket!" screamed Dan,
"Well... I haven't found mine, it could be anywhere"
Said Rat, "How about you, Snake, old man?"

"I've found one! I've found one!... Look, under thisss rug!"
Yelled Snake as he crawled into view,
"And I've got mine," smiled Olly, "it was inside a mug,
Now Skinny and Frog... that leaves you!"

Within minutes they'd managed to find ***all*** *the parcels,*
There was paper all over the place,
"Well, that was tremendous fun Matty, you rascal!"
Said Frog, a huge grin on his face.

The party continued... it was full of fun things,
Pass the parcel... Pin the tale on the mule,
Hide and seek... Christmas Carols (everyone had to sing),
Even Rat, who felt such a fool!

Dan

By the time they all sat down to eat they were shattered,
Matty handed them all party hats,
"Well, mine's far too small," joked Frog, "but no matter,
Dan and I will just swop! How about that?"

"What a super spread, Matty," said Eel eyeing up the food,
All the mince pies...and trifles and tart,
"Can I begin?," enquired Moorhen, "or is that being rude?"
"No, you dig in," said Matty, "Go on! ***Start!****"*

Throughout the whole meal the house echoed with laughter,
There were stories...and jokes...and lots of gossip,
"Tonight we'll remember for many months after,"
Rat winked, as he took another sip.
"It'sss a pity to end sssuch a fantastic evening,"
Snake said sadly, glancing out at the snow,
"But I sssuppose fairly soon we'll all have to be leaving,
I, for one, will be sssorry to go!"
"Yes, I think we should gather our boots and our coats,
And start heading for home," Frog agreed,
"But let me say my dear Matty, before we all go,
It was splendid...thank you very much indeed!
I know I can speak for everyone here,
This has been THE BEST CHRISTMAS PARTY EVER!...

...So now, let's all wish you
A HAPPY NEW YEAR,
AND MAY WE ALL REMAIN GOOD FRIENDS
...FOREVER!"

THE END